things I th

written by emma mccabe

cover art by eden biggs

Dedication:

To Dad, Mom, Cj, Audrey, and Aidan–

You are the greatest gifts I know in this life.

Thank you for the way you love me.

These words are for you.

things I think about when I drive

by emma mccabe

Remember that feeling you get when the summer day was a scorcher from morning until night, until suddenly it wasn't? Until it's 8 PM and you're sitting in a bathing suit still, dried to your body, under a massive sweatshirt because if you never get up off the sand, the day is never over, it's summer forever.

Every night in my dreams I remember the way it feels to wake up in delight. Maybe I'll bike to the market to wander around with a coffee and pick out the perfect peonies to bring home, to bathe them in sunlight on my windowsill, to mix their scent deliciously with the candle I bought six months ago. Or maybe I won't! Maybe I'll throw an obnoxiously fun dinner party with disco balls and champagne and my mom's chocolate cake and everyone invited has to wear a cowboy hat and perform stand-up comedy.

I'll throw on a pair of tennis shoes and race you to the ocean. You promise me you'll swim and I'll jump in without looking back. I'll pull a one dollar paperback out of my bag and read until the pages and my hair are dry and then I'll race you back to the water again. I'll spend the rest of the day praying that I can make it as a writer, and you'll be praying for rain for your tomatoes.

Four years ago I bought a book secondhand because I liked the title and I forgot about it until I moved out of my parent's house and finally remembered to clean out my box from that summer. On the inside cover, in pencil, someone, a boy from the handwriting, had scribbled "because this is the only way I can make sense of things. call me when you finish it" and now for the rest of my life I have to wonder if she called him and what the novel revealed to her. Each chapter made me cry and now I'll never be able to get over the story I wrote in my head about the people who loved this book and I'll love that story more than anything else. And it'll never be finished and it'll never be written.

I've loved the Beatles since the first time I heard "Hey Jude" and heard them screaming so achingly beautiful that I thought all of their lungs would burst. And then I loved them even more when my dad was driving me down the coast, next to the beach, as fast as the ocean, and they crooned "Golden Slumbers" to me and I thought I was living. And then it was a deeper love, when I watched them on my screen trying again and again and again to perfect "Dig a Pony" but they could never get anything done because they were having so much fun and I wanted to grasp that fun with my hands and hold it close. And I'll love them forever, as their songs are the soundtracks of my days, are the sounds of my most treasured memories, but I'll never love them more than when I close my eyes and press play on "Dear Prudence".

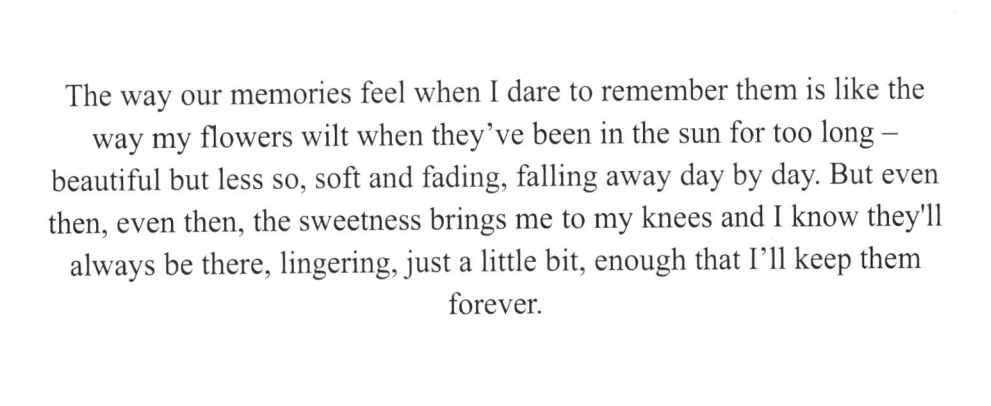

The way our memories feel when I dare to remember them is like the way my flowers wilt when they've been in the sun for too long – beautiful but less so, soft and fading, falling away day by day. But even then, even then, the sweetness brings me to my knees and I know they'll always be there, lingering, just a little bit, enough that I'll keep them forever.

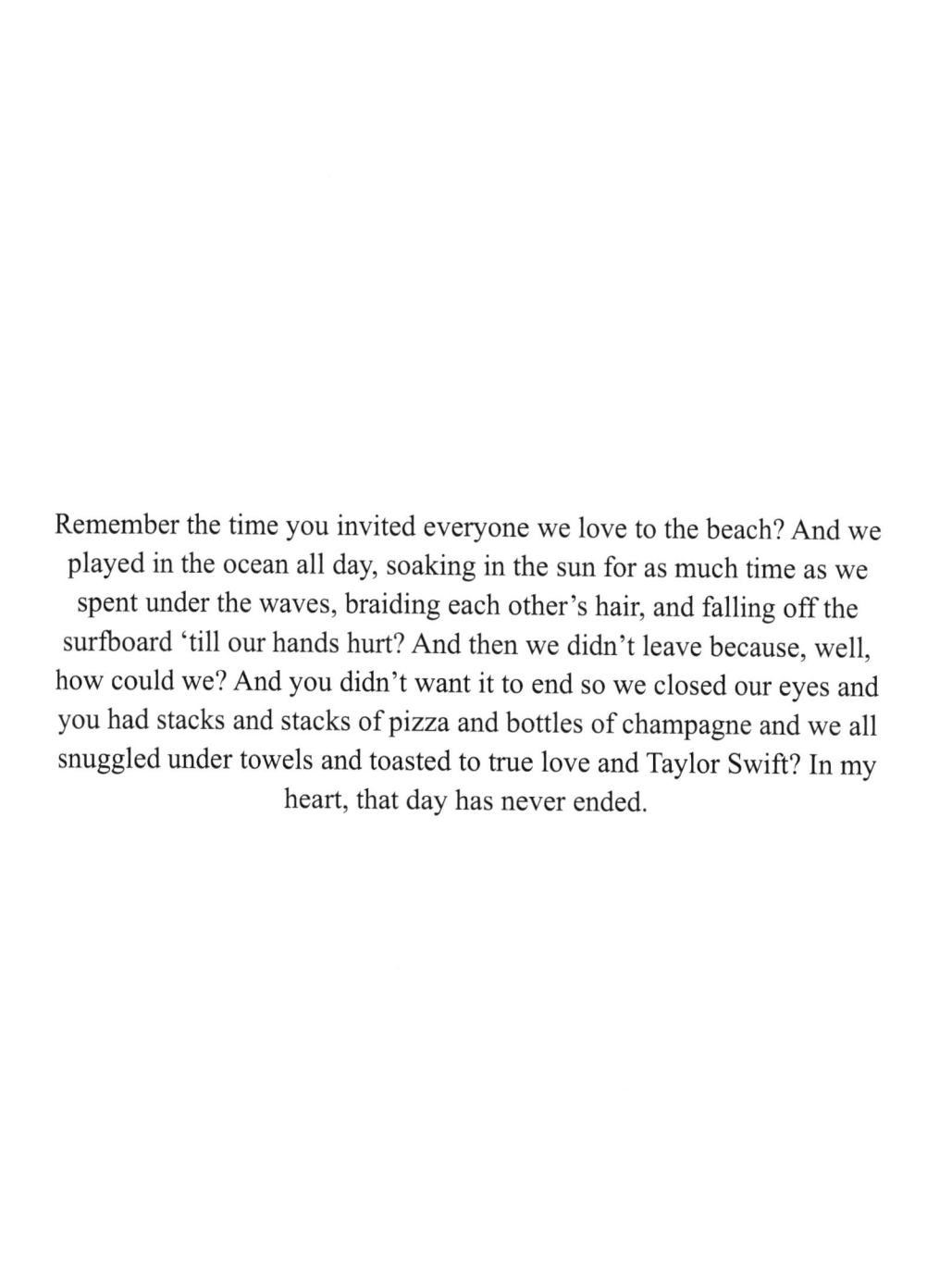

Remember the time you invited everyone we love to the beach? And we played in the ocean all day, soaking in the sun for as much time as we spent under the waves, braiding each other's hair, and falling off the surfboard 'till our hands hurt? And then we didn't leave because, well, how could we? And you didn't want it to end so we closed our eyes and you had stacks and stacks of pizza and bottles of champagne and we all snuggled under towels and toasted to true love and Taylor Swift? In my heart, that day has never ended.

I was fifteen the first time I remember being embarrassed by how much I loved to read, when I felt the shame seeping into my chest because I preferred books to so-called cooler things, and I didn't want to tell anyone because I didn't want it taken away from me, and I couldn't bear to have it tainted. And the dread deepened until one day I was freed because what is cool anyway? And ever since then, for the sake of fifteen-year-old me, who I protect with every single breath, I carry a novel with me everywhere I go, and recommendations roll daintily off my tongue. I make homes in the libraries and bookstores nearby and take refuge amongst the pages. And now I pray every night that you protect your fifteen-year-old self, too.

When I write about you I don't write about the things you said to me, how your breath catches right before you start laughing, or how we liked all of the same music and that freaked me out. I write about the way my knees felt when you asked me to dance. I write about how before I knew we were going to be at the same party I used to fidget with my necklace until you walked in the room and my hands knew peace. I write about the way my heart was broken when you pretended to forget things I told you and I tried to stop telling you things after that. I write about how I miss you, not often, but on days when I know you'd be outside, smiling at the sky, happy to be here, just like me.

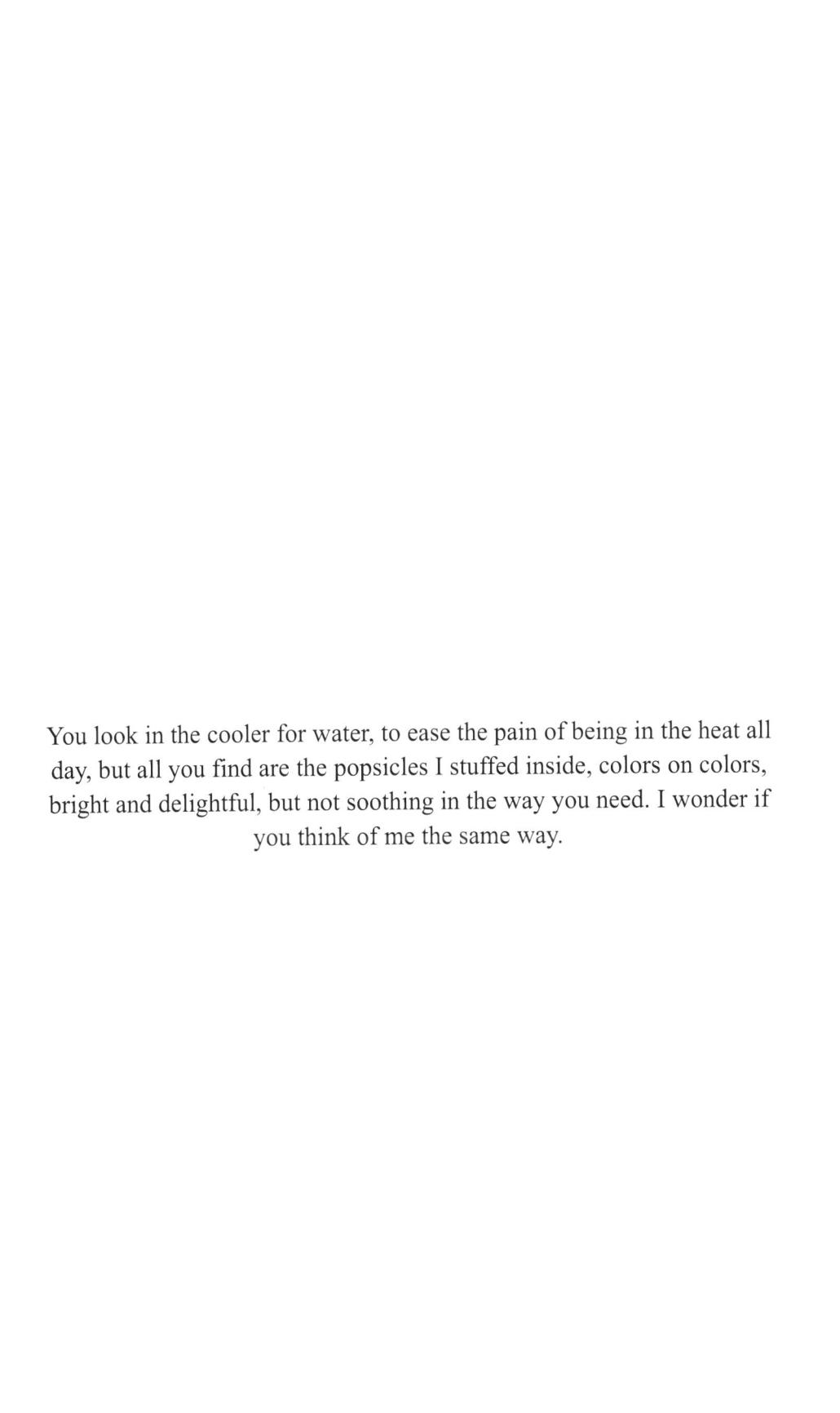

You look in the cooler for water, to ease the pain of being in the heat all day, but all you find are the popsicles I stuffed inside, colors on colors, bright and delightful, but not soothing in the way you need. I wonder if you think of me the same way.

My sister asked me last summer what I dream of when I let myself and I didn't have an answer, didn't trust myself to throw something out haphazardly, not when somehow I knew the words I said would define me forever. A summer later I looked at her tenderly and said, "I dream of peace in my heart, an ocean to run to, a hand to hold, and a book I get to write".

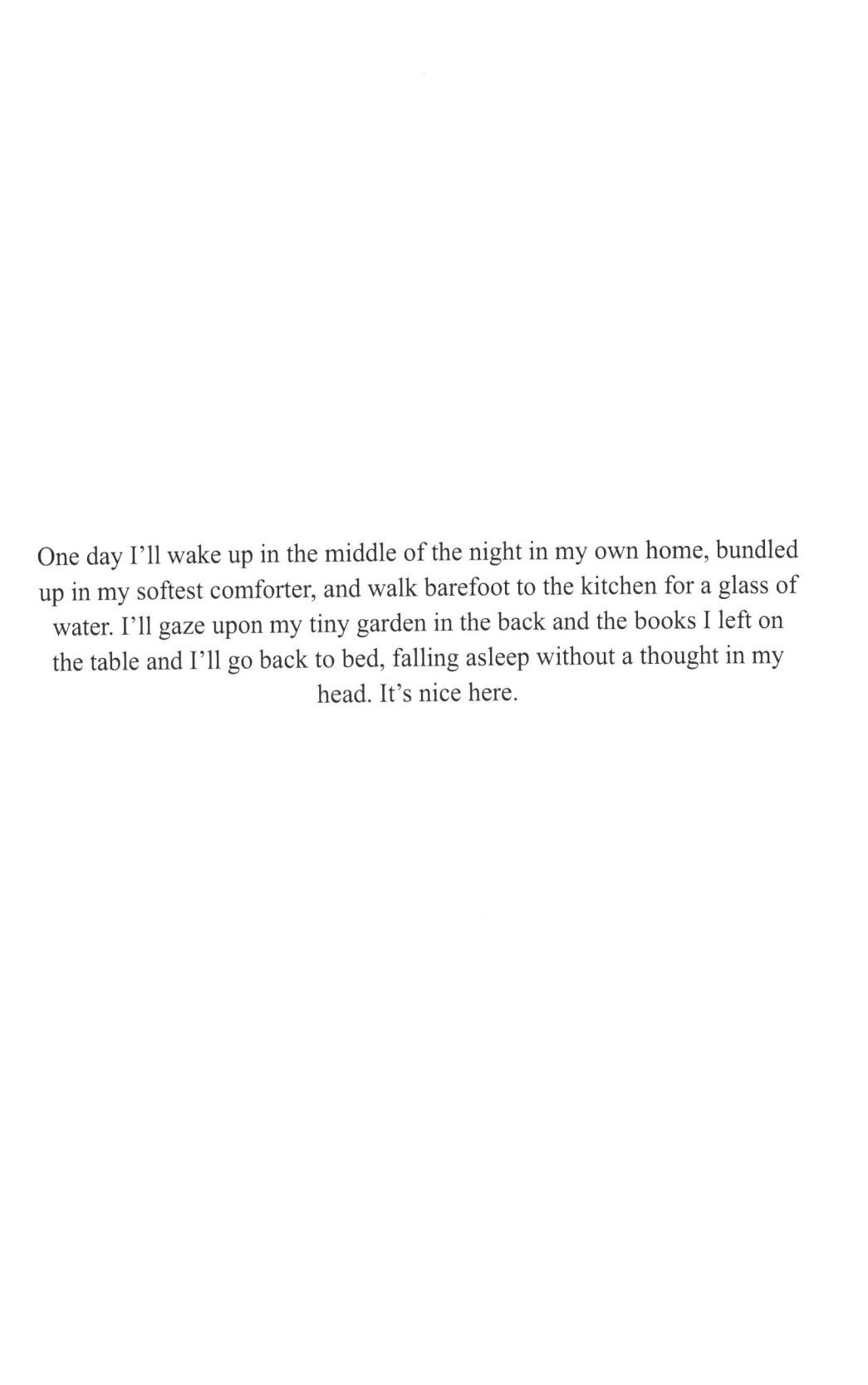

One day I'll wake up in the middle of the night in my own home, bundled up in my softest comforter, and walk barefoot to the kitchen for a glass of water. I'll gaze upon my tiny garden in the back and the books I left on the table and I'll go back to bed, falling asleep without a thought in my head. It's nice here.

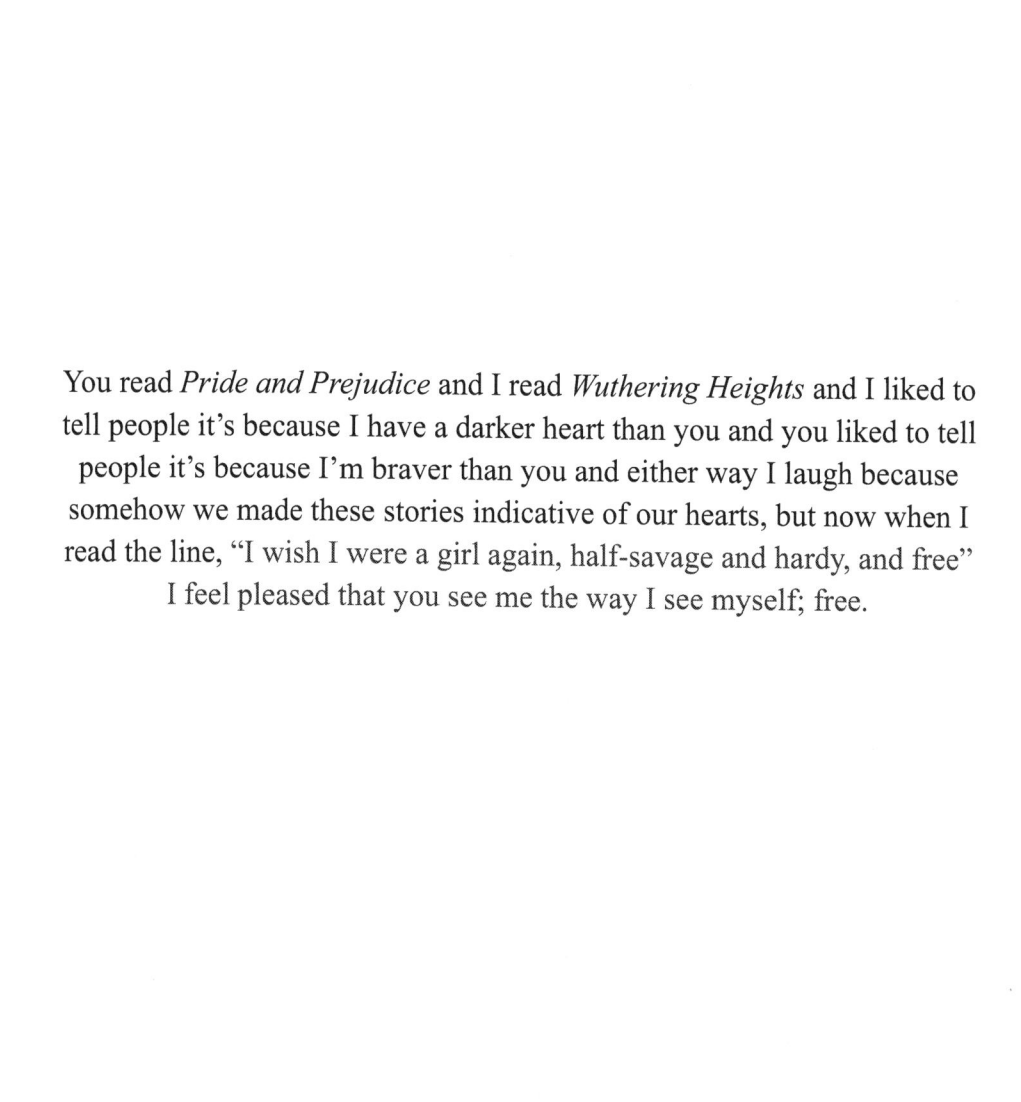

You read *Pride and Prejudice* and I read *Wuthering Heights* and I liked to tell people it's because I have a darker heart than you and you liked to tell people it's because I'm braver than you and either way I laugh because somehow we made these stories indicative of our hearts, but now when I read the line, "I wish I were a girl again, half-savage and hardy, and free" I feel pleased that you see me the way I see myself; free.

It's spring and my heart is breaking

Or, rather–

It's spring and for the first time I don't wonder what life would be like without you

My heart is breaking is a roundabout way to say

I know myself now and wreckage has to occur to be filled up with something beautiful

Which means that maybe I'm cracked wide open

So that the light can pierce my heart and rearrange my head

Some days I wander around with my head in dreamworld

Occupied with late afternoon swimming in the ocean or the butterfly I saw leaving work last week or the sentence I read in the Oscar Wilde book last year

And I force myself to be ripped back to reality

Because dreaming is not productive

Until I sit down to match pen with paper

And everything makes sense again and I can see clearly

And it's the one place I feel like I don't need to be anywhere else

And I write about my heart being ripped to shreds by Jane Austen because it makes sense here

I wandered through confusion and doubt

Hazy days where upside down was reality

Backwards was the way everything made sense in my head

Chest tight, wringing hands, thoughts on loop on loop on loop

Then one day suddenly the fog was clear

I could see again and more importantly–

Dream again

And the work that felt like my constricting my heart suddenly made sense

We made pasta close to midnight and then ate it off of my grandmother's vintage china. We sat in the soft glow of the moon with all of the lights off and rather desperately I thought, oh God, I think I'm in love with you. You reached out to hold my trembling hand and now whenever I make pasta or peer at the moon on a rather glorious night I have the same intrusive thoughts again and my mind can't stop saying oh no oh no oh no I'm still in love with you.

A list of things I'd include if I ever wrote you a love letter:

A spray of my everyday perfume

A poem by Mary Oliver ripped out of my favorite book

A lengthy description of the roses I'm growing in my garden

A paragraph of my thoughts on *Anna Karenina* and my despair about learning a new language

A silk ribbon taken from my jewelry box because I love the texture

A single sentence on how befuddled I feel when I'm around you

A sonnet on saying goodbye

Prayer comes to me in different forms; the Lord is gently speaking to me. Sometimes it is a quiet thought, to be repeated when I pray in church, or on the pages of my journal. Often it is a walk by the water, the sun gently going to sleep for the evening. Occasionally it is from the lips of strangers, more often from the mouths of my best friends. But no matter what, no matter how it looks, it means the Holy Spirit is moving, roaming freely in my heart and my life, a tendril of hope for me to follow all of my days.

A peony scented candle flickers in the corner as you write, hunched over the journal your mother gave you ten years ago. The fountain pen attacking the page mercilessly, flawless cursive overwhelming the dainty yellow pages. An edge of stillness sits in the air, the world leans over to watch, silently, never disturbing, as magic itself is created. You lean back eventually, wringing the pain out of your hands, rubbing ink accidentally on your forehead, exhausted from the effort of pouring life into pages, and close the notebook. Night resumes.

Once upon a time I wore a dress that fluttered over the grass, with puffed sleeves, and the picture of romance. I tucked a flower behind my own ears and you watched, pleased. What are you looking at, I asked. The way you idolize the ordinary, you laughed. I frowned, mystified. What's wrong with making every moment beautiful. Nothing my love, you smiled, no one sets the world on fire like you do.

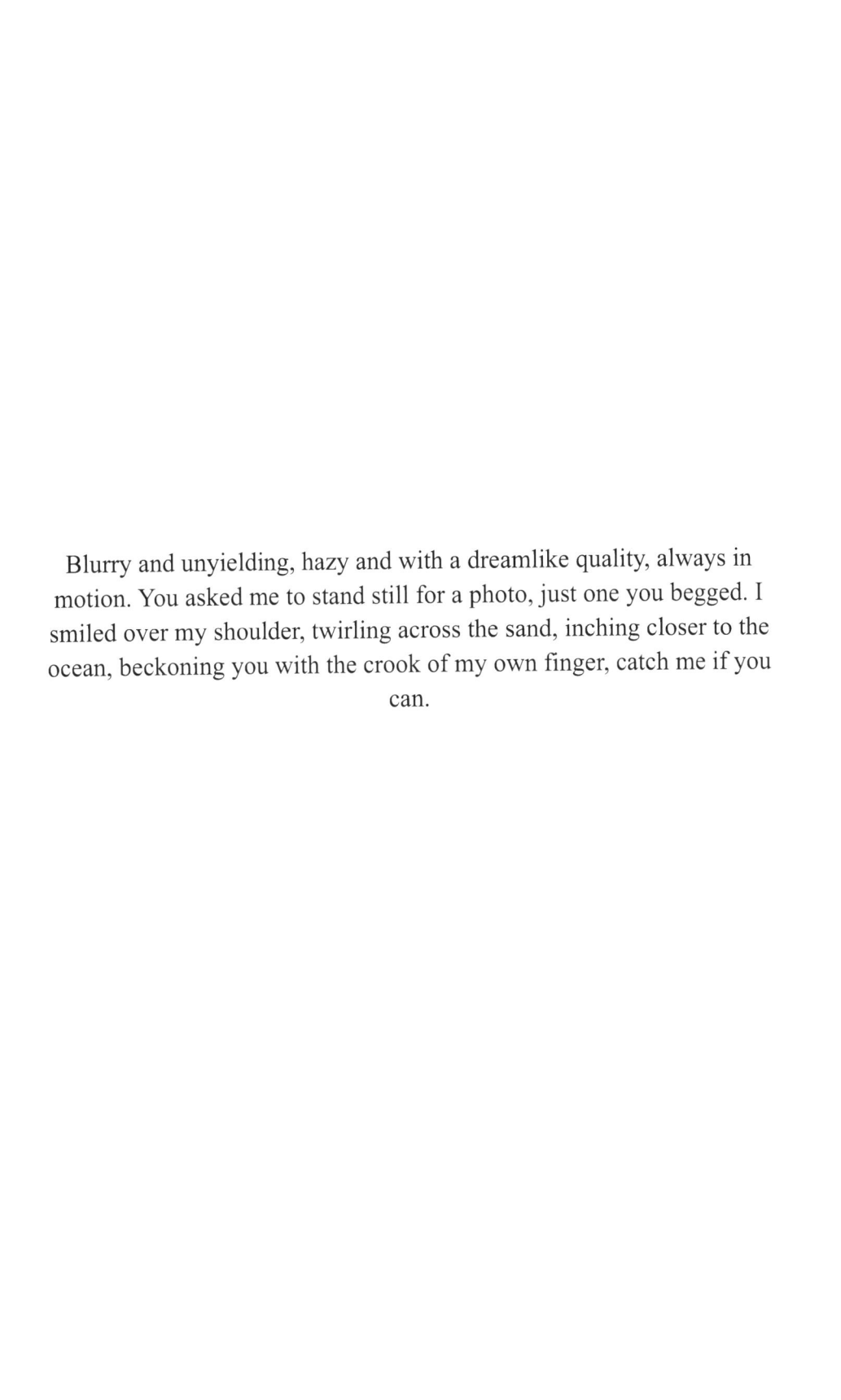

Blurry and unyielding, hazy and with a dreamlike quality, always in motion. You asked me to stand still for a photo, just one you begged. I smiled over my shoulder, twirling across the sand, inching closer to the ocean, beckoning you with the crook of my own finger, catch me if you can.

There was a boy who loved a girl very much. He tried for years to show her his heart without laying it all on the table. He was always her knight in shining armor, without the goodnight kiss. The one who answered the midnight calls, the dashing date when her plus-one failed to show, the family man who her little brother adored, the purchaser of her favorite flowers and bottle of wine. Until one day when another man got down on one knee, before he knew what was happening, before he could stop it, and she raised a dainty hand to her mouth, proclaiming gladness. And the wickedness of it destroyed him a little bit, stole the air from his lungs, and he had to watch her walk down the aisle to a man who wasn't him.

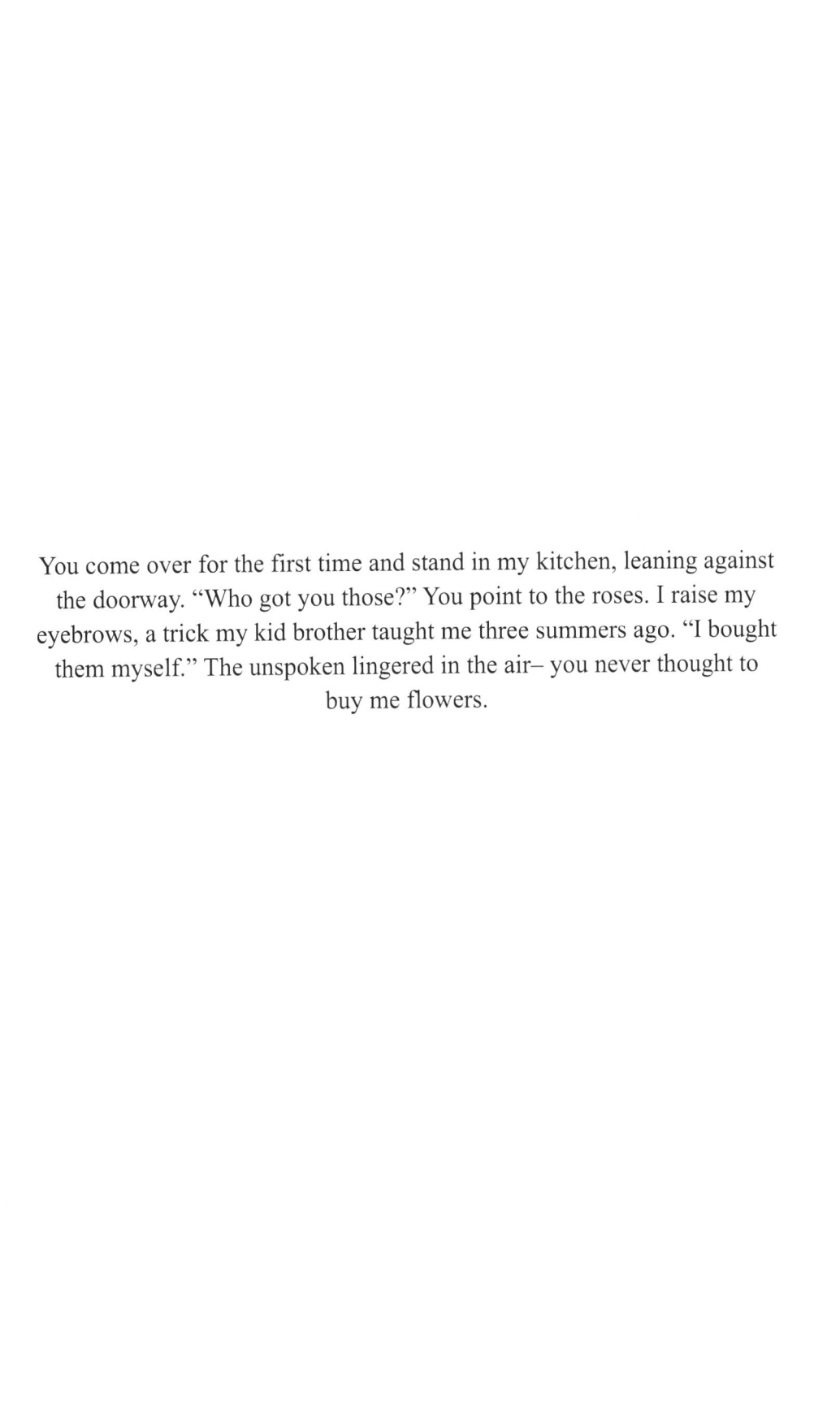

You come over for the first time and stand in my kitchen, leaning against the doorway. "Who got you those?" You point to the roses. I raise my eyebrows, a trick my kid brother taught me three summers ago. "I bought them myself." The unspoken lingered in the air– you never thought to buy me flowers.

The grocery list of the week is as follows:

Kindness, for breakfast

Flowers, for dinner

Chocolate cake, to drop at the neighbors

Red wine, to drink on the beach

One box of pens, to write you love letters forever

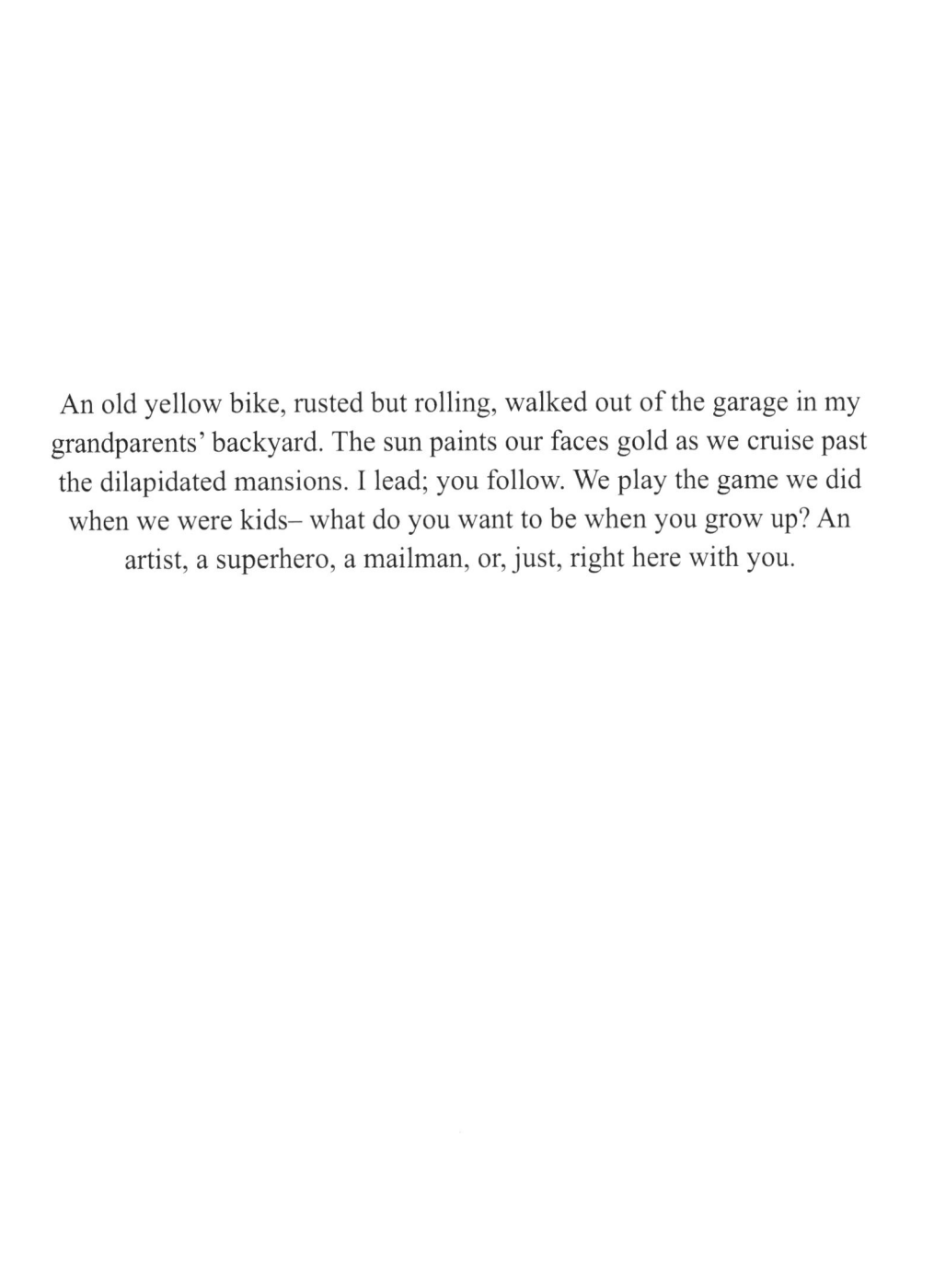

An old yellow bike, rusted but rolling, walked out of the garage in my grandparents' backyard. The sun paints our faces gold as we cruise past the dilapidated mansions. I lead; you follow. We play the game we did when we were kids– what do you want to be when you grow up? An artist, a superhero, a mailman, or, just, right here with you.

Brown nails, perfectly shaped, long tan legs, dark hair twisted up curly and wet. Flopped down on the towel, blue and white striped, elegant and classic. Twisting the earrings in your right ear, back and forth, until your restless hands stop. A hat pulled low over your eyes. The ocean behind you, raging and angry.

Read your books

Drink your wine

Surf your wave

Pick your flower

Write your song

Perform your dance

Just – be where your heart tugs you

I broke your heart but you broke mine first and now we can't think of each other without remembering the night under the moon where everything was lost for good but I must tell you – I think of all the other nights, too.

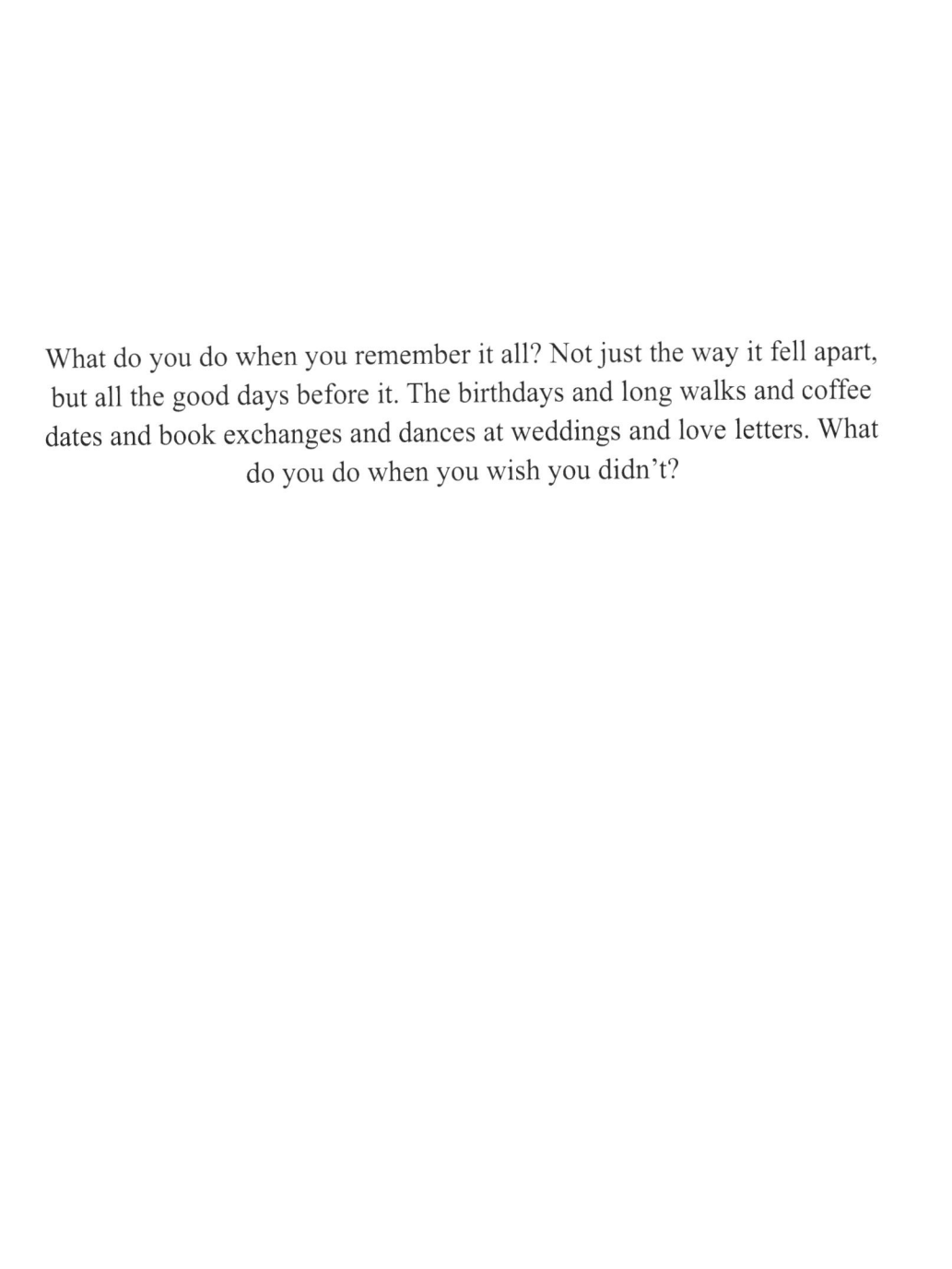

What do you do when you remember it all? Not just the way it fell apart, but all the good days before it. The birthdays and long walks and coffee dates and book exchanges and dances at weddings and love letters. What do you do when you wish you didn't?

You're my favorite hand to hold

A superior taste in music

Beach days where the waves are gentle

Bottles of champagne that pop and fizzle

The first sunburn of the summer

A long car ride

A place to call home

I want to lay in the ocean when it's stiflingly hot outside, float on the surface, and close my eyes. Let me rest here a little longer.

I set my books down on the sleek, gray surface. My hands cup the mug of steaming hot coffee. The rain pours outside the window. I'm protected by the glass, only, and the warmth of my caffeine. The overhead bell chimes as the next customer walks in; friendly greetings are exchanged across the shop. I look up and we lock eyes. My heart sinks. We don't know each other anymore.

I'm teaching myself to lean into what brings me joy and lean away from what hurts when I can avoid it. Self care.

We got glasses of champagne and sat under painted skies. The symphony created art for our ears only. I wore an orange dress with ruffled sleeves and dreamed about a future where I created art for a living. We laughed until our ribs cracked and then laughed some more. When fear crept in, art saved our lives.

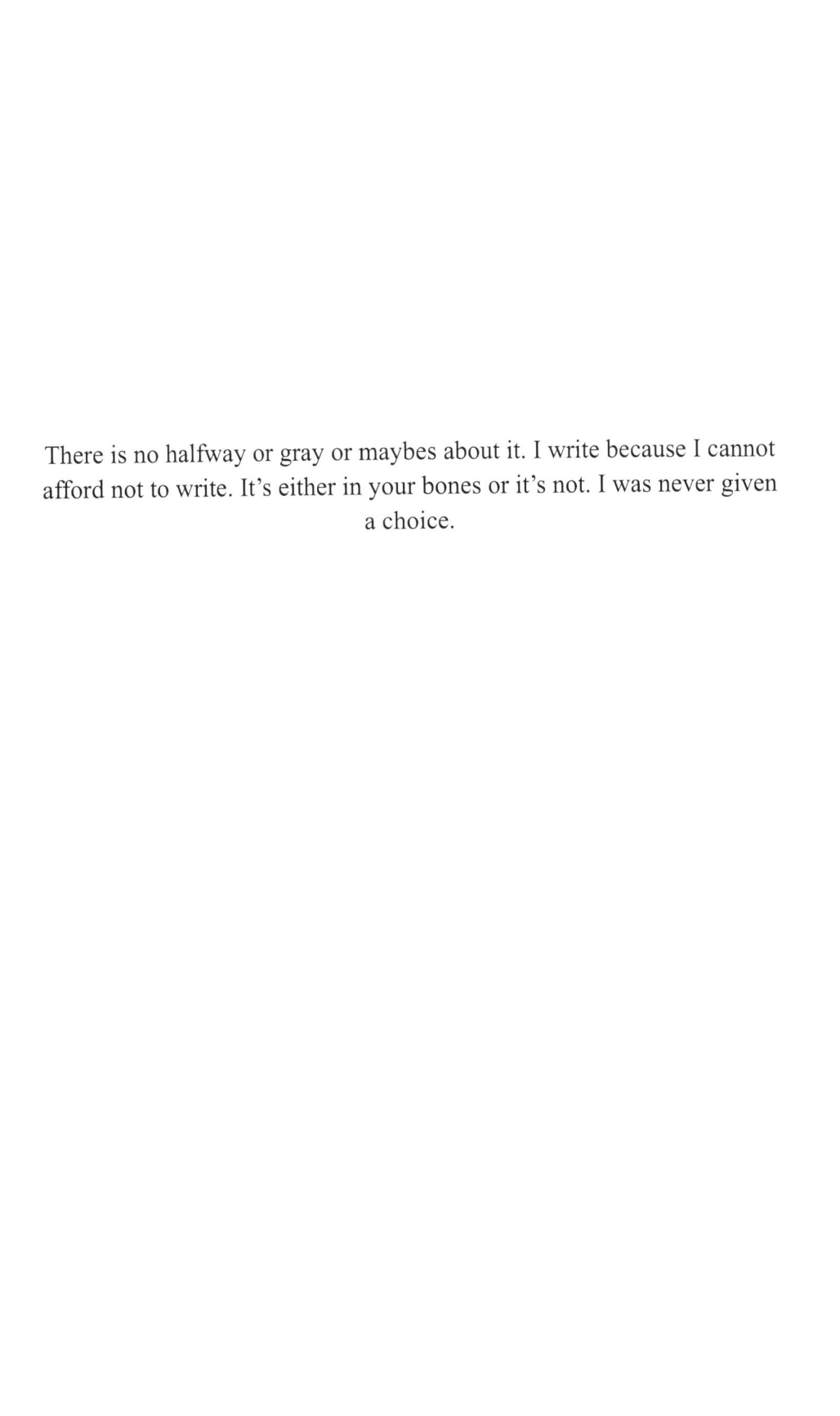

There is no halfway or gray or maybes about it. I write because I cannot afford not to write. It's either in your bones or it's not. I was never given a choice.

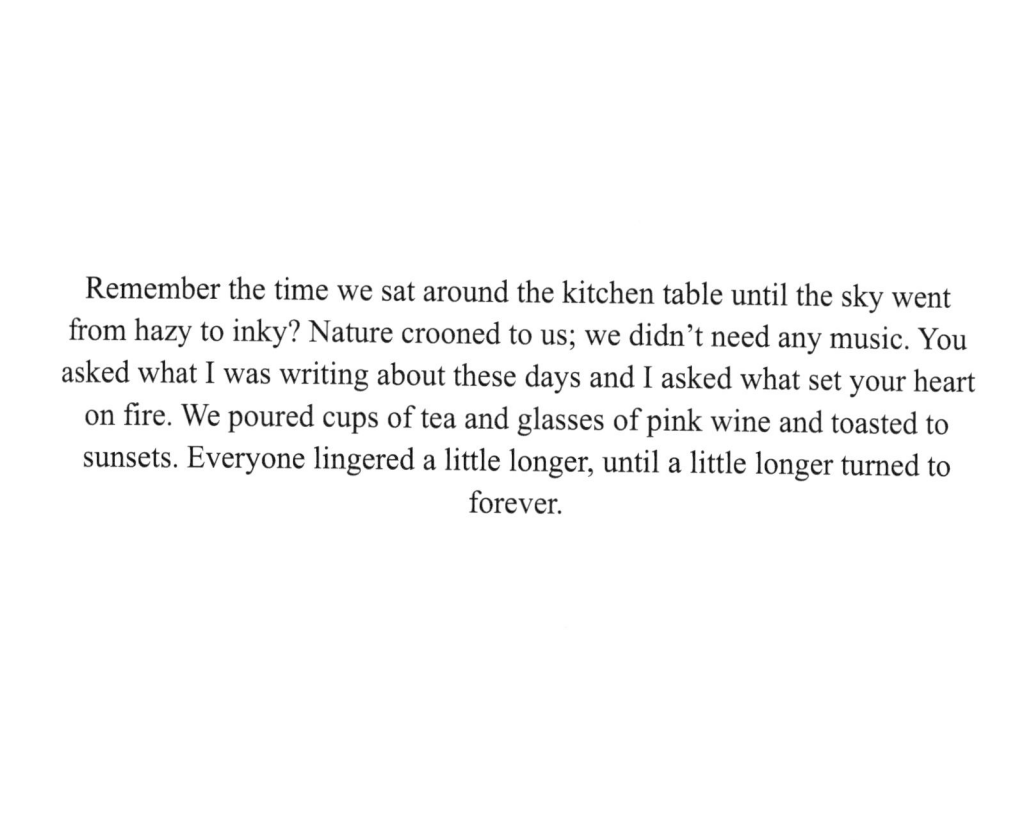

Remember the time we sat around the kitchen table until the sky went from hazy to inky? Nature crooned to us; we didn't need any music. You asked what I was writing about these days and I asked what set your heart on fire. We poured cups of tea and glasses of pink wine and toasted to sunsets. Everyone lingered a little longer, until a little longer turned to forever.

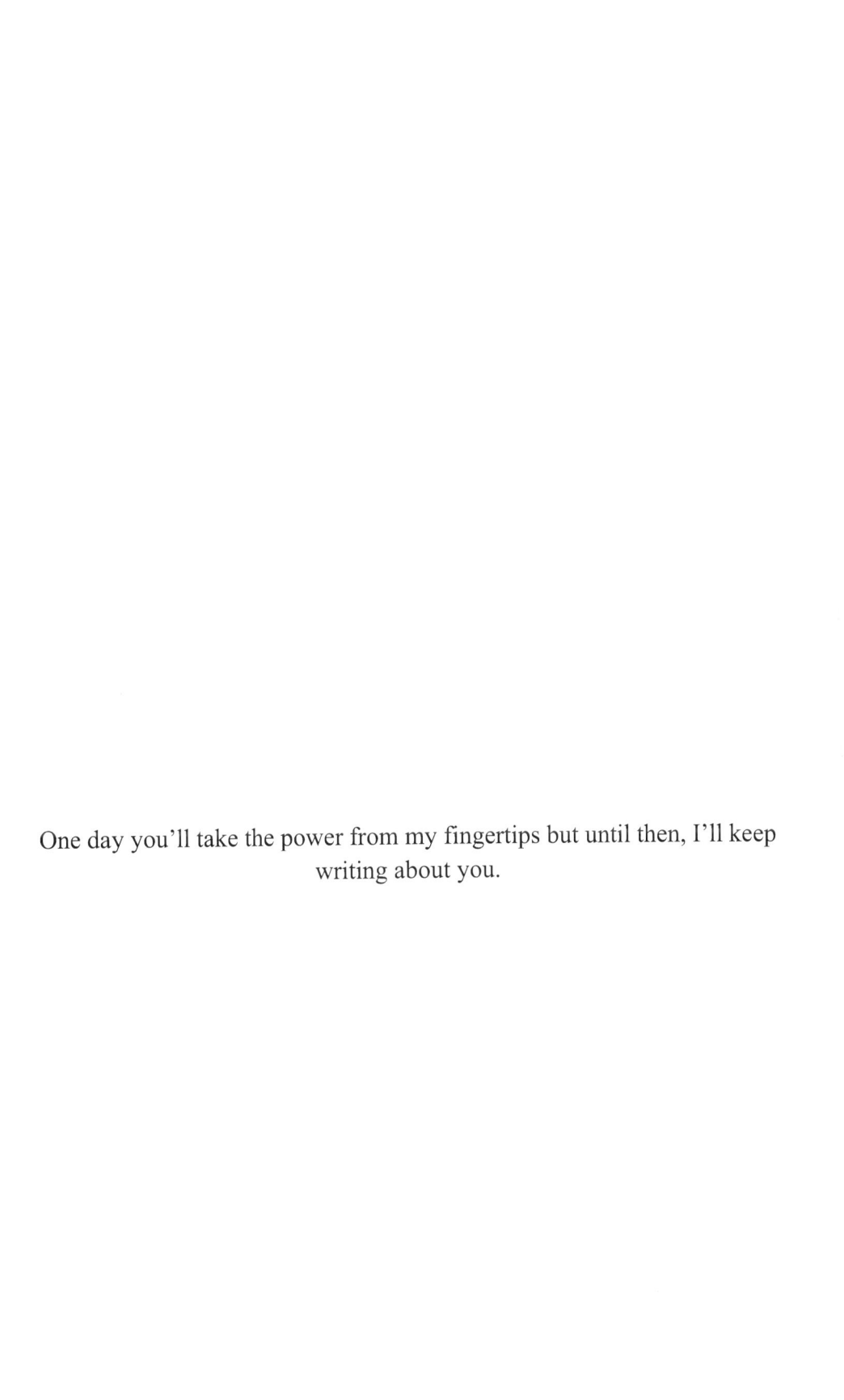

One day you'll take the power from my fingertips but until then, I'll keep writing about you.

Kindness abounds. Joy repeats. Grace saves.

Keep this in your pocket.

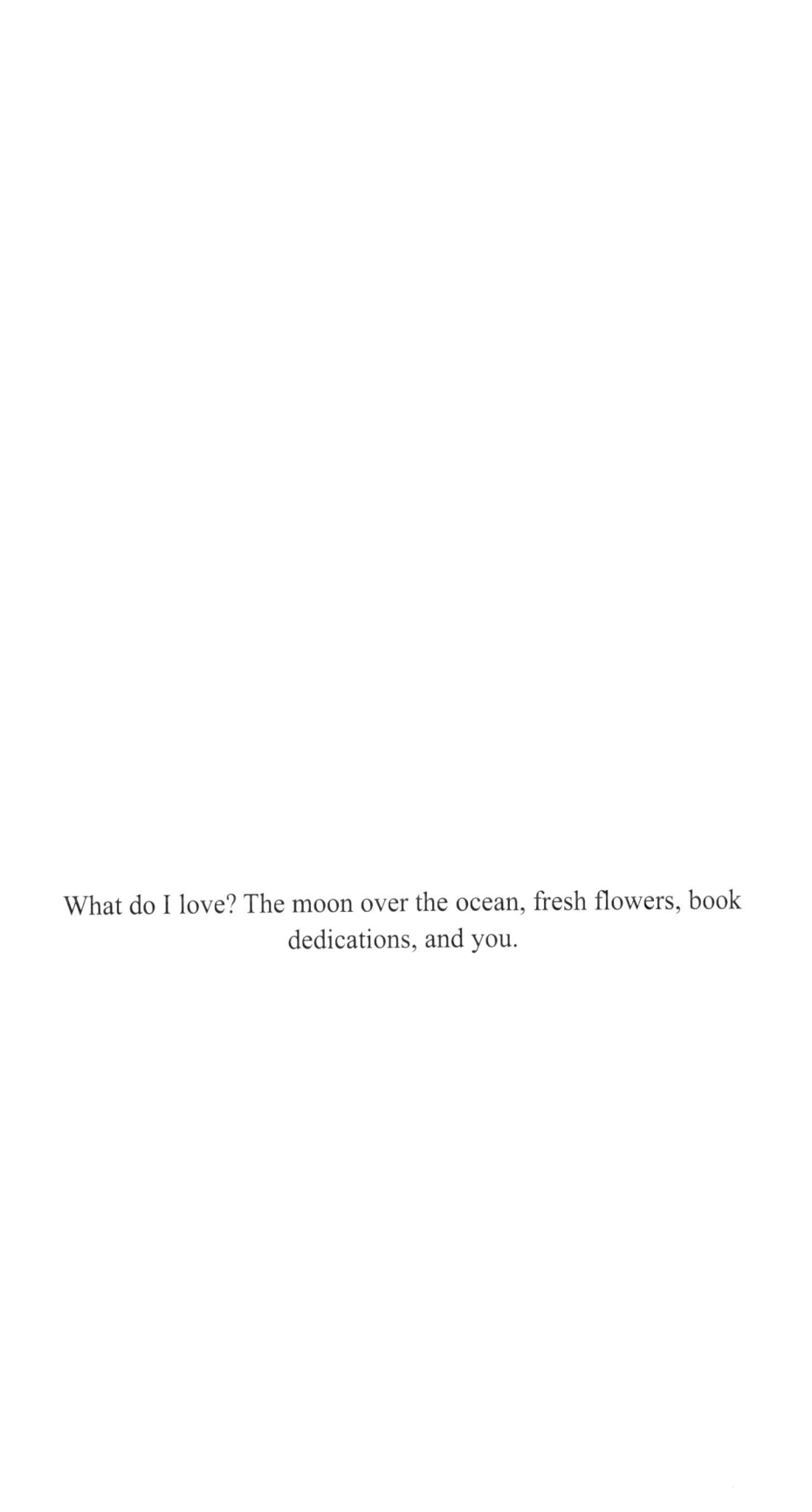

What do I love? The moon over the ocean, fresh flowers, book dedications, and you.

I've come to realize lately that what I thought is not true–
Screen time and competition and busy makes me feel nothing but blue

And what I lost along the way is what I'm looking for right now
Friendliness and time outside and play are what matter anyhow

Kickball and four square and evening swims in the sea
Card games and love letters and dinners where my friends sit across from me

These are the things that fill my heart with tender joy
Rather than what the world tells me, that which feels like a ploy

It's a season where my heart feels cracked into pieces
And though change is hard, the fear continually decreases

Grab my hand and let's make ourselves a pact
To live life this summer where we all make eye contact

We'll go on long walks and host tea parties and have a movie marathon
Sit at breakfast with phones tucked away and lay blankets on the front lawn

I'll keep choosing you and you keep choosing me
And at night I'll drink my peppermint tea balanced on my knee

I'm waving a fierce goodbye to half-hearted and muddled and muted
Prayer and freedom is where you'll find me rooted

As a girl who is known for having a lot of big feelings—

You magnify everything in my heart

Trust me when I say it wasn't easy to be broken by you

Aesthetic:

I save old pictures tinged with yellow

Underline book quotes with glee

Keep a box of my favorite ribbons

Send bottles of champagne for events worth celebrating

Write poetry about boys who broke my heart and also about the ocean

Collect bookmarks from places I'll never go again

Buy enough coffee to last me a lifetime

Have confetti in my back pocket in case of a rainy day

Watch romcoms and family favorites by night

Pray in the light of an early morning

And all that to say–

I work hard to to seek joy, because sometimes she hides

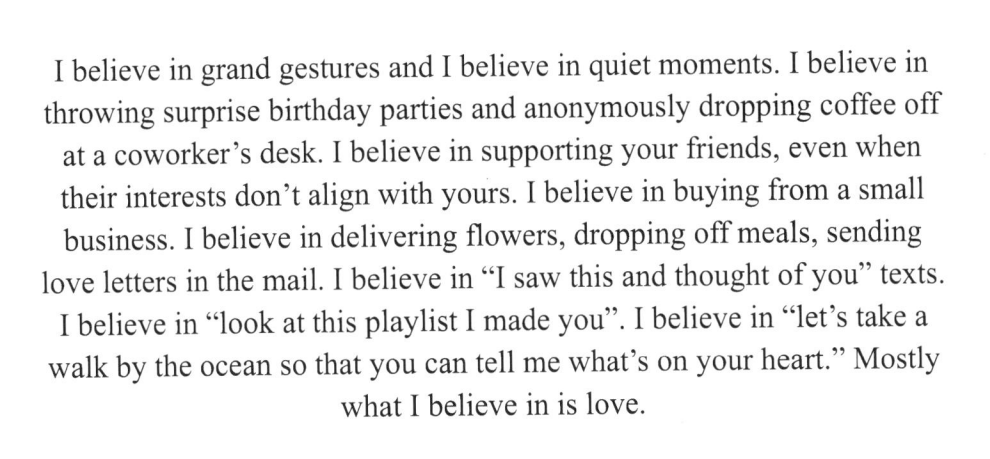

I believe in grand gestures and I believe in quiet moments. I believe in throwing surprise birthday parties and anonymously dropping coffee off at a coworker's desk. I believe in supporting your friends, even when their interests don't align with yours. I believe in buying from a small business. I believe in delivering flowers, dropping off meals, sending love letters in the mail. I believe in "I saw this and thought of you" texts. I believe in "look at this playlist I made you". I believe in "let's take a walk by the ocean so that you can tell me what's on your heart." Mostly what I believe in is love.

You never read my writing, which is probably a good thing. Because it's always about you.

June is the way it feels to sleep in late on a Saturday, to roll over and see light peeking through the curtains, knowing you are completely rested. It's lazy smiles over iced coffees. It's reading English novels in the park on a blanket next to your sister. It's the way it feels to swim in the ocean at 7 PM, as if nothing else exists but you and the waves. It's white sheets and a golden bed frame. It's the chirping of birds at 7 AM as you leave for work and everything around you is green and alive. It's wine and cheese parties with your neighbors and cups of tea with your grandparents. It's the way your heart feels when you snuggle with a puppy. It's dancing under disco balls at midnight. It's flying through book after book on the beach and not moving all day, baking in the sun. It's driving in tune to the sunset listening to a playlist your best friend made you when you were sixteen. It's the smell of honey, the smell of lavender, the smell of salty ocean air. It's wearing long dresses with puffed sleeves and feeling like the picture of whimsy but all you're doing is running to the grocery store. It's sending your college roommate a surprise bottle of wine in the mail. It's the way it feels when you let go of the swings midair and fly for a moment before crashing back down to Earth. It's rinsing off in an outdoor shower in your bathing suit, sand crusted to your body. June is romancing your own heart, showing her how it feels to be taken care of.

Twenty-Three

There is no feeling on Earth like the sun warming your skin
Or listening to your favorite song again and again

Except maybe the time when I was twenty-three
And found out all of the world believed in me

They sang my name in high-pitched tones
I felt myself growing, I felt it in my bones

First I had to stretch to grasp the stars
Until I realized they were never that far

And then I went dancing all through the night
Whirling and twirling to everyone's delight

Sometimes I like to remember the look on your face
From the time that I told you it was never a race

Now when I dream it's me that I see
A girl who is kind, who is happy to be

So on the nights when I am tired or lonely or cold
I can hear them all whispering, "what a wonder to behold"

My tears are my guide:

This hurts me

This brings me joy

This tenderness is too much to bear

This surprises me

I put ribbons in my hair so that you know my heart is gentle. I keep my nose in a book so that you know my heart is adventurous. I write jokes on sleeves of loose-leaf paper so that you know my heart is funny. I wear my heart on my sleeve so that you know I adore you.

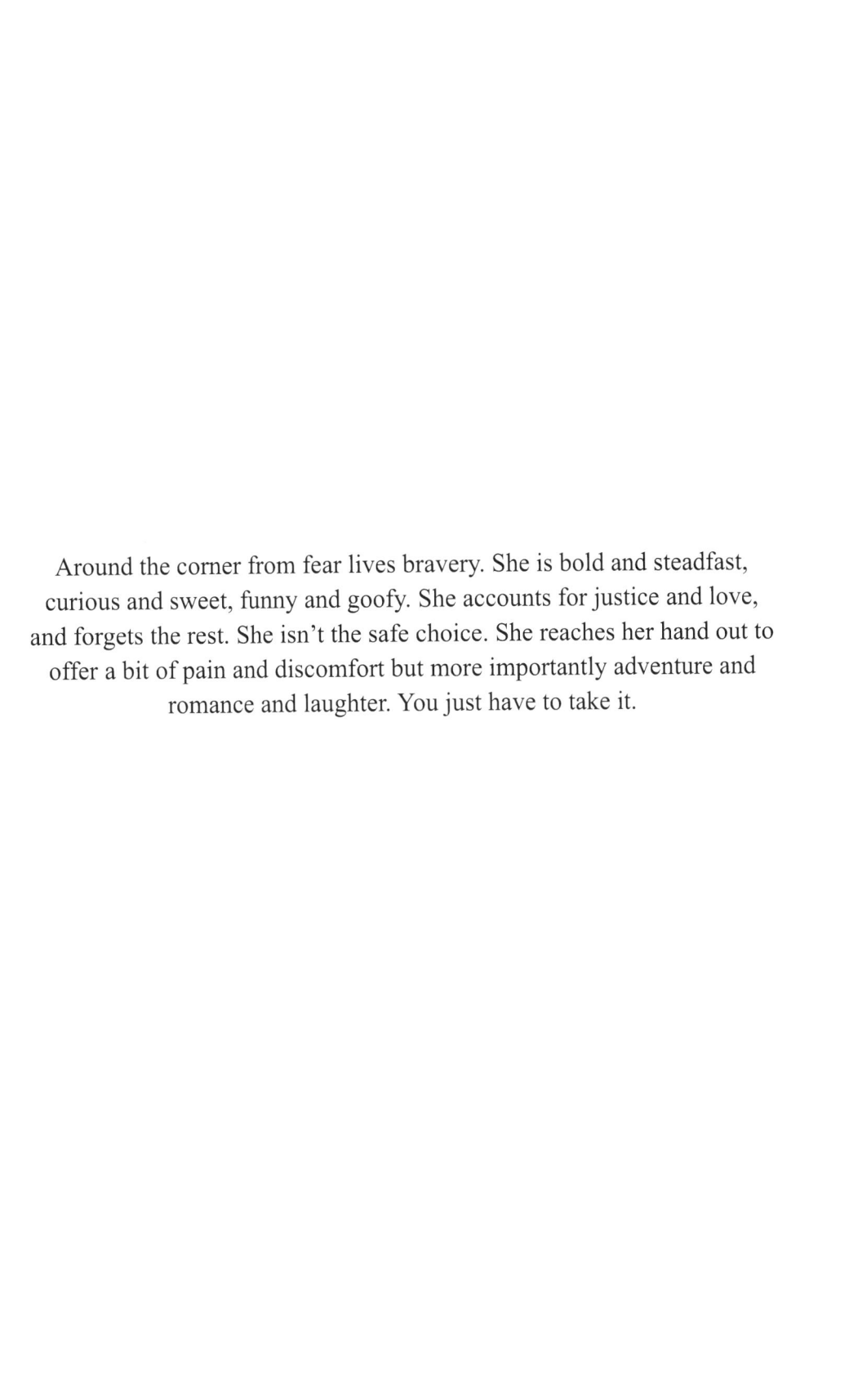

Around the corner from fear lives bravery. She is bold and steadfast, curious and sweet, funny and goofy. She accounts for justice and love, and forgets the rest. She isn't the safe choice. She reaches her hand out to offer a bit of pain and discomfort but more importantly adventure and romance and laughter. You just have to take it.

Kickball:

There are no days I love like I love this day
When all my friends meet at the park to gather and play

It's not unusual to see costumes and masks and ribbons and pearls
Summer friendships of young and old, of boys and girls

We rarely keep tallies or scores or count up the innings
But everyone who goes home takes with them the winnings

Popsicles are handed out and new memories created
Enough to carry us through winter when we sat and waited

Four summers long of oversized t-shirts and greasy pizza slices
A place to forget the world when we are left to our own devices

I am welcome, and so surely are you
And your mom and grandmother and neighbor and boss, too

We run a kickball league truly in name only
But we are really in the business of making others less lonely

When the days are hot, the skies are clear, and the sun is setting
You'll find us in a place that we'll never be forgetting

Heartbeats:

Pulsing, every second of every day

Calmly, steadily, routinely

Until–

You

Speeding up, double time, over time

My hand to my chest, as if I am in control, can stop it, can calm it

My words, once mesmerizing, are all at once:

Silly and unrefined and breathless

The pitter patter of my beating heart against my ribcage

Can be heard across the world

But you–

Don't even notice

You and the Ocean

You and the ocean

Intertwined in my mind

As vast as you are shallow

As see-through as you are hazy

One moment

I'm drowning

The next

Floating, peacefully

You threaten to sweep me under

Wreck me thoroughly

You caress my cheek gently

A whisper of your power

Frazzled and floundering

I fight to keep my head above the waves

Expose me and save me

You and the ocean

Winter:

The sound of the wind keeps me company on my way to you
Whistling and dancing and flirting on demand

Beams of light from the moon guide my path
When they fall on me it's like I'm thrown in a warm bath

I pass shop windows– dazzling and majestic and shiny and bright
The one dash of humanity on this freezing cold night

Church bells sound in the distance to usher in the new day
Clanging and banging to their neighbor's dismay

Peace settles on my heart as the familiar comes in creeping
And I wonder what you dream of in your head while you're sleeping

The silence and the stillness are the soundtrack of my thoughts
They weave their way inside to untangle all of my knots

As the night wanders on, crisp and perfect and waning
Beauty strikes again, still here and still reigning

I'd walk forever to keep this gentleness in my soul
But it's not 'till I arrive that I feel safe and I feel whole

Peace:

I searched high and low
I ran to and fro

My legs began to grow weary
My eyes were all teary

The heart said no more
Leave your hope at the door

And then He came knocking
And said, let's get to talking

"Beloved, you have been searching in all the wrong places
It will not be found in faraway lands or in new faces

Idols and treasures will not a man make
You can earn and earn and your heart will still ache

This thing that you chased, that you seeked and you craved
Was given long ago, the way already paved

You are loved more than you know
And because of that, I took the blow

I'll sit by you all night
And watch as your fears finally take flight

And now that you see, rest easy, rest free
Sit on the banks under the shade of the tree"

Summer Heart:

There is beauty in this season
& in the heart of our summer girl

Her golden jewelry glints in the sun as she floats in the ocean
Everything is bright & hazy & blinding
The sun
& the way she just shines

She is all Light-
Goodness overflowing out of her like the sunsets she chases

She is all Love-
Pure and wholesome like the books she devours on the sand, day after day

When the little moon finally comes out to play, you will find her with a glass of champagne
Or throwing dinner parties where everyone is invited & no one is a stranger

She may even be sleeping hard on sheets the color of grass
But it's only because she gets up with the sun
& starts her day with coffee & the lull of the waves

You may know her by the love notes she leaves behind her
Or by her laugh--uninhibited & infectious

One day I'll write a story about her
My protagonist
Who is fierce & fun & free
She'll break your heart a million ways to Sunday
But you'll love her anyway

But for now I'll leave her to be
Laying in the grass & dreaming of the beach

He wrote me a love letter that went just like this--

On Monday there was a rainbow right over the sea

On Tuesday a stranger paid for my coffee

On Wednesday the butterflies came back to play in my garden

On Thursday my mom played tennis with me until the sun went down

On Friday an old friend sent me a letter in the mail

On Saturday I filled the last page of my very favorite journal

And on Sunday in church He smiled at me through the light in the stained glass windows

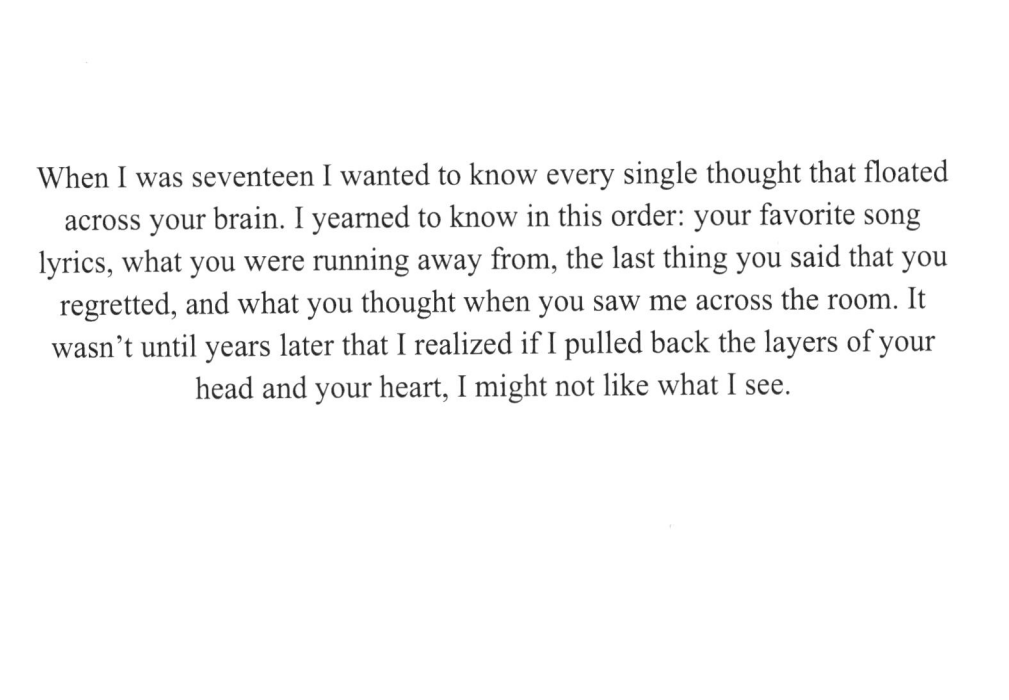

When I was seventeen I wanted to know every single thought that floated across your brain. I yearned to know in this order: your favorite song lyrics, what you were running away from, the last thing you said that you regretted, and what you thought when you saw me across the room. It wasn't until years later that I realized if I pulled back the layers of your head and your heart, I might not like what I see.

Whimsy:

In the throes of ordinary life, I had forgotten the meaning of play
Too quick to say no; too eager to seem wise

The mountains of Colorado looked me square in the eyes
And demanded my attention, keeping anxiety at bay

A dear friend took my hand and turned the volume way up loud
And we sprinted from coffee shop to book store and back home again

I resisted the pull away and get lost in the crowd
Throwing off the chains of who I might have been

I remembered laughter and eagerness and kindness and love
Picking flowers, writing poetry, wearing overalls, and drinking warm wine

And when God said what's next? I gave stiffness a shove
Saying yes to a life where everyone has the chance to shine

I never knew that wandering through the wreckage of a lost season could feel strangely like everyday life. Running through the rain for a cup of coffee, getting yourself out of bed for yoga, trying each night to come up with something new to write in a journal feels normal even when you are wandering around with your eyes closed. As you and I fumble for the light, let's do so with grace. Amongst the bittersweet days of change, we are found and bound by our love.

Words:

The world makes sense to me in words and by that I mean when I'm sad I don't say I'm sad, I say I'm devastated because I need you to know the weight that words carry. When I say I'm proud of you, I say you are every good thing on this planet and my heart explodes when I look at you because I can't believe I get to know you and watch you shine because to just say I'm proud would be a disservice to your light. Simple sentences fall flat to me because then I'm reaching and yearning for more-- I don't want you to tell me today was fine when really today was beautiful and heart wrenching and you spilled coffee on yourself on the way to work but your favorite barista smiled at you so you forgot about the coffee. Gestures and facial expressions are fine, but I need to know what rips your heart to shreds and what causes it to do cartwheels. Words are the way I grasp and fumble my way through my existence on Earth.

I dream of a place where I am free to be
It might be little, cozy, and facing the sea
You come to visit me there sometimes
When it's been a long day and you need to unwind

I serve champagne in coffee mugs
And am always waiting to welcome with hugs
There are books on the table, stuffed into corners, anywhere they can fit
We lay on the floor and finish puzzles with grit

I throw loud parties with confetti and bare feet
We eat cake and laugh and everything is sweet
I grow out my hair, long and tangly and brown
And when it's your birthday, I force you into a crown

There are more blankets than the eye can see
And outside of my bedroom window is a big and billowing tree
The doors are flung wide open and we paint them light green
And when we dance in the kitchen, I feel like I'm fifteen

I hope it's a place where people come to linger
And every joke that is told is always a zinger
We'll learn lots of things, like French and how to bake
And even when things are hard, they will never ever break

The garden will be rambling and lush and wide
There will be peonies and roses and hydrangeas inside
The mailbox is stuffed with poems and love letters
And every winter we watch the sunset in thick sweaters

This little house will be a place to come pray
A cottage where you will always feel welcome to stay
And if you want to know if you can come too
I'll be at the door saying, "I've been waiting for you"

Follow me to the creek–

Where flowers dance and ripples sing

We can jump in from the top of the rock

Like we're kids again

Let's sun our bodies on the grassy shores

While clouds gently drift over us

I'll pass you a bottle of water

You'll pass me a book of poems

When the sun goes home for the night

We can make our trudge back to reality

We'll tuck this day in our back pocket

For when we need to remember simplicity

This Must Be The Place:

When my mind wanders off to faraway places
Lately, it's been this moment I cling to–

Green as far as the eye can see
Feeling small in a world brimming with delight
Perspective; what seems to matter up here?
Wispy clouds floating by, gently dropping water on me

Apples that make a crisp sound when I bite into them
Listening intently to the sound of my own heartbeat
Wonder fighting to take up its place in my life
A release of control; the desire to lay around for a while

I see the paths of wildflowers like a map guiding me home
Joy thrives here, the place between heaven and earth

Sitting in a candlelit room watching the rain destroy the world outside. Comforted in a midnight green pajama set and a mug of steaming hot peppermint tea. Reading a series from my childhood for the millionth time. Peace eternal.

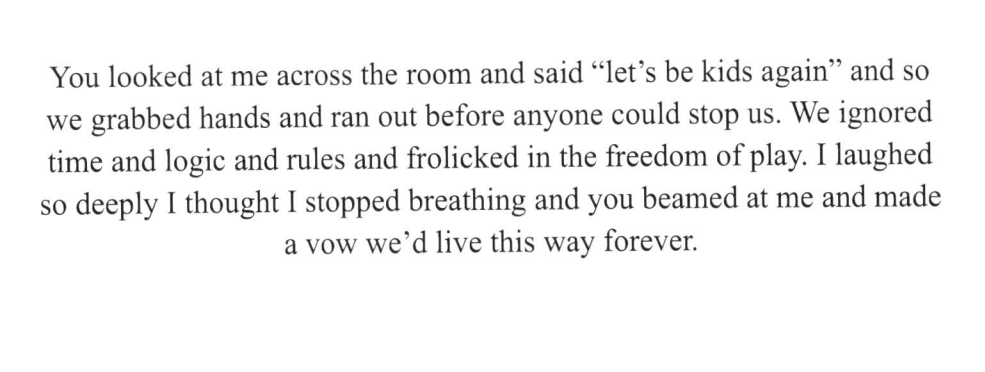

You looked at me across the room and said "let's be kids again" and so we grabbed hands and ran out before anyone could stop us. We ignored time and logic and rules and frolicked in the freedom of play. I laughed so deeply I thought I stopped breathing and you beamed at me and made a vow we'd live this way forever.

Four summers ago we wrote each other letters across the country and I wrote about the way my dreams cracked my ribs open and you wrote about the way music had completely changed your life and every day, even when I felt like we'd never been further away, I knew we had never been closer. Now when you read in the same room as me, or when I play that one song in the car, we exchange wry smiles, knowing those letters were the start of the great love affair of our lives.

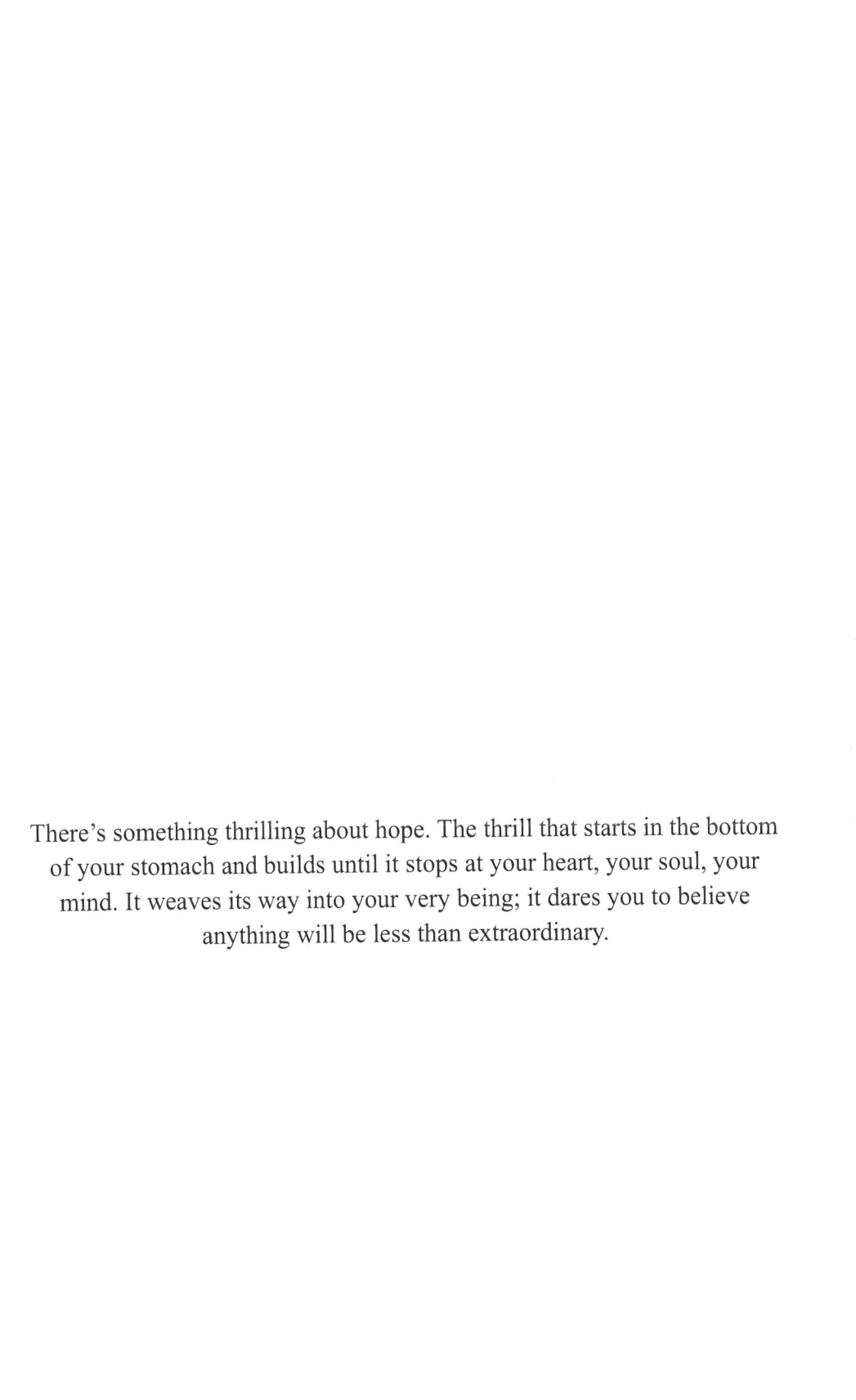

There's something thrilling about hope. The thrill that starts in the bottom of your stomach and builds until it stops at your heart, your soul, your mind. It weaves its way into your very being; it dares you to believe anything will be less than extraordinary.

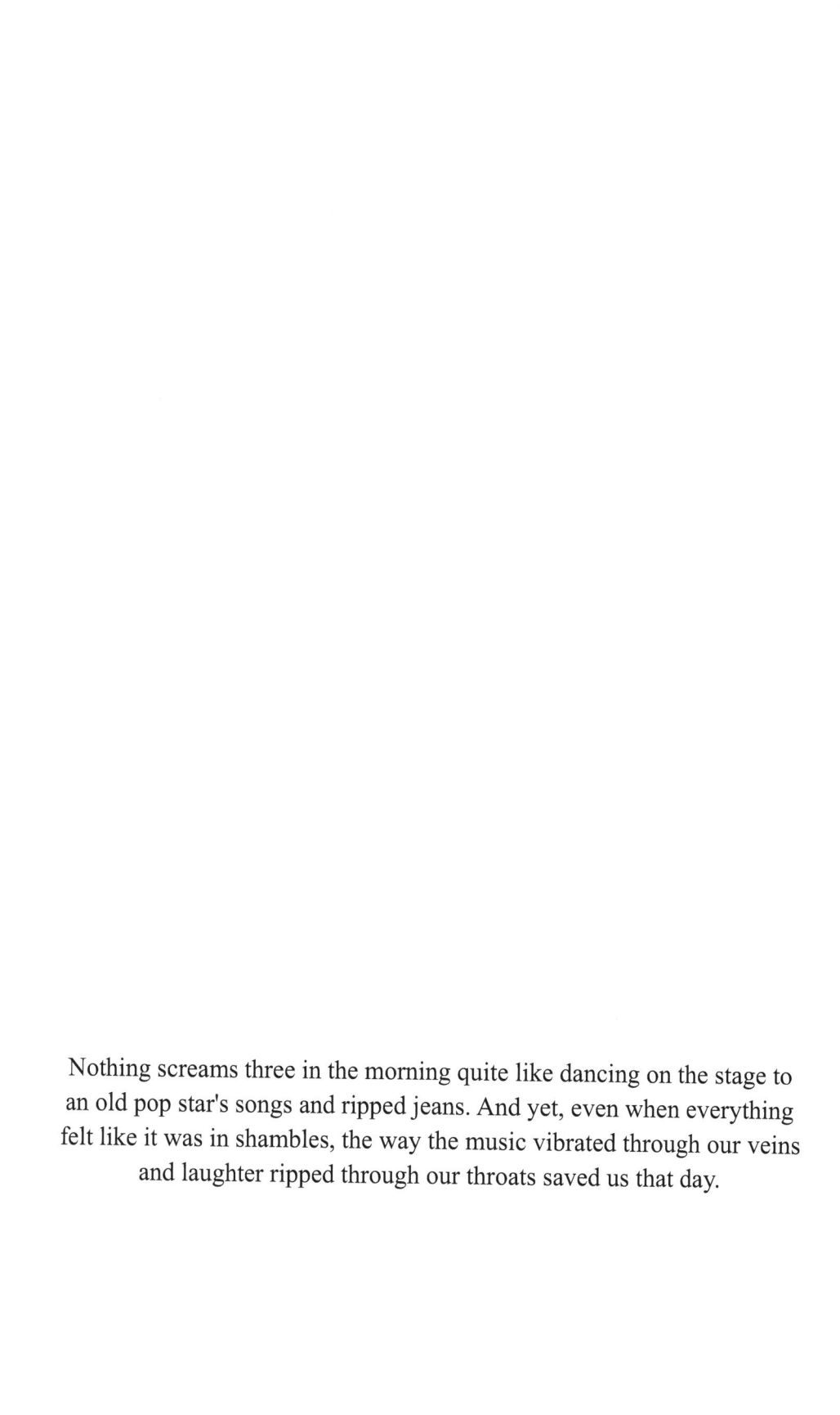

Nothing screams three in the morning quite like dancing on the stage to an old pop star's songs and ripped jeans. And yet, even when everything felt like it was in shambles, the way the music vibrated through our veins and laughter ripped through our throats saved us that day.

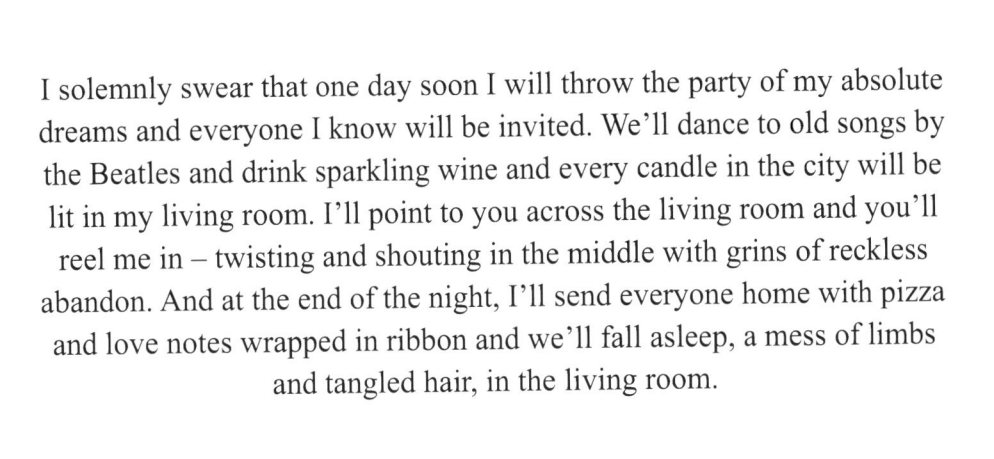

I solemnly swear that one day soon I will throw the party of my absolute dreams and everyone I know will be invited. We'll dance to old songs by the Beatles and drink sparkling wine and every candle in the city will be lit in my living room. I'll point to you across the living room and you'll reel me in – twisting and shouting in the middle with grins of reckless abandon. And at the end of the night, I'll send everyone home with pizza and love notes wrapped in ribbon and we'll fall asleep, a mess of limbs and tangled hair, in the living room.

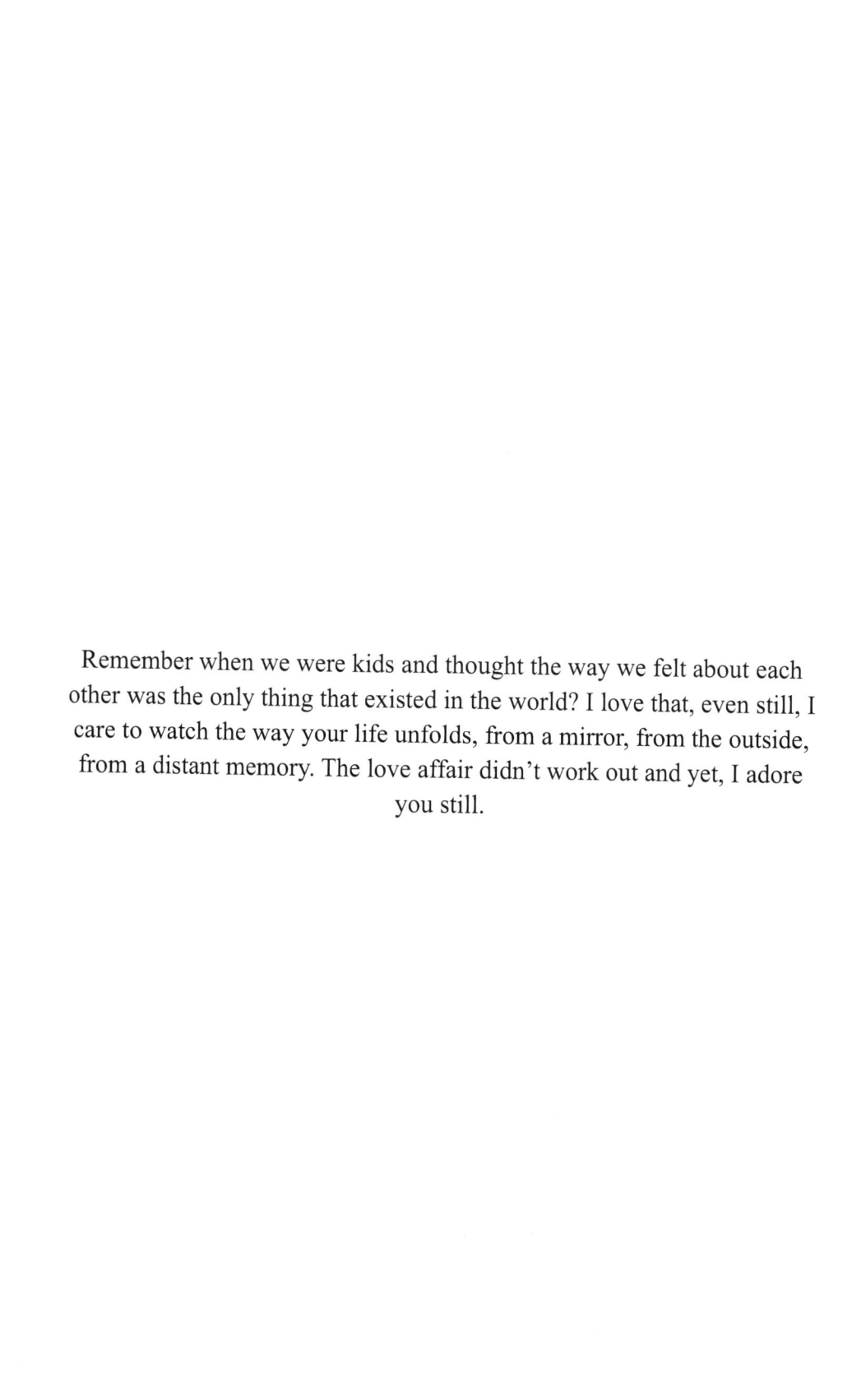

Remember when we were kids and thought the way we felt about each other was the only thing that existed in the world? I love that, even still, I care to watch the way your life unfolds, from a mirror, from the outside, from a distant memory. The love affair didn't work out and yet, I adore you still.

Thunder cracking overhead

Fat droplets blinking in our eyes

Dark clouds, signs of warning

But we only saw the ocean

And each other

Nervous giggles as we sprinted from sand to water

Plunging our bodies into the waves

Linking hands so we didn't drift away

Unceasing storm

Lightning far off in the sky

Tan skin in the blue water and blinding smiles

Nothing exists but this moment

Joy eternal; I'll dream of it forever

The day we swam in the rain—

And forgot the rest of the world

Summer feels like beating your older brother in a game of cards, sitting on the back porch, drinking a glass of red wine right as the sun goes down. It's wearing cardigans over sundresses to walk on the beach at dusk and throwing your hair in a sloppy ponytail when the heat gets to you. It's fresh flowers and fresh lemonade and fresh romance. It's wearing all black and accessorizing with glinting golden jewelry. It's devouring paperback after paperback and creasing the pages after you read a line that tugs on your heart. It's watermelon in bright blue dishes and sweating cups of iced coffee. Summer feels like diving into a wave and letting the freedom of it wash over you.

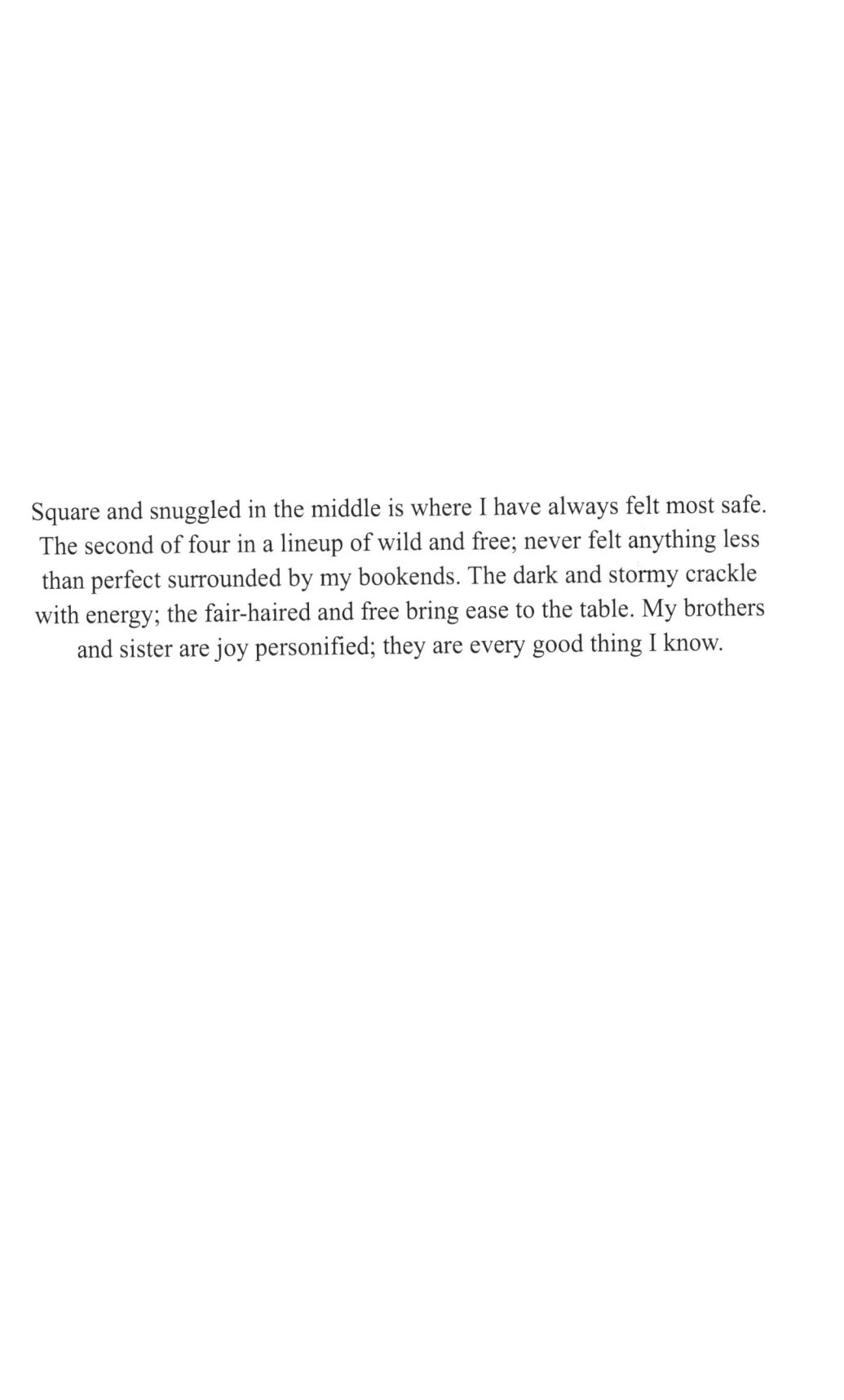

Square and snuggled in the middle is where I have always felt most safe. The second of four in a lineup of wild and free; never felt anything less than perfect surrounded by my bookends. The dark and stormy crackle with energy; the fair-haired and free bring ease to the table. My brothers and sister are joy personified; they are every good thing I know.

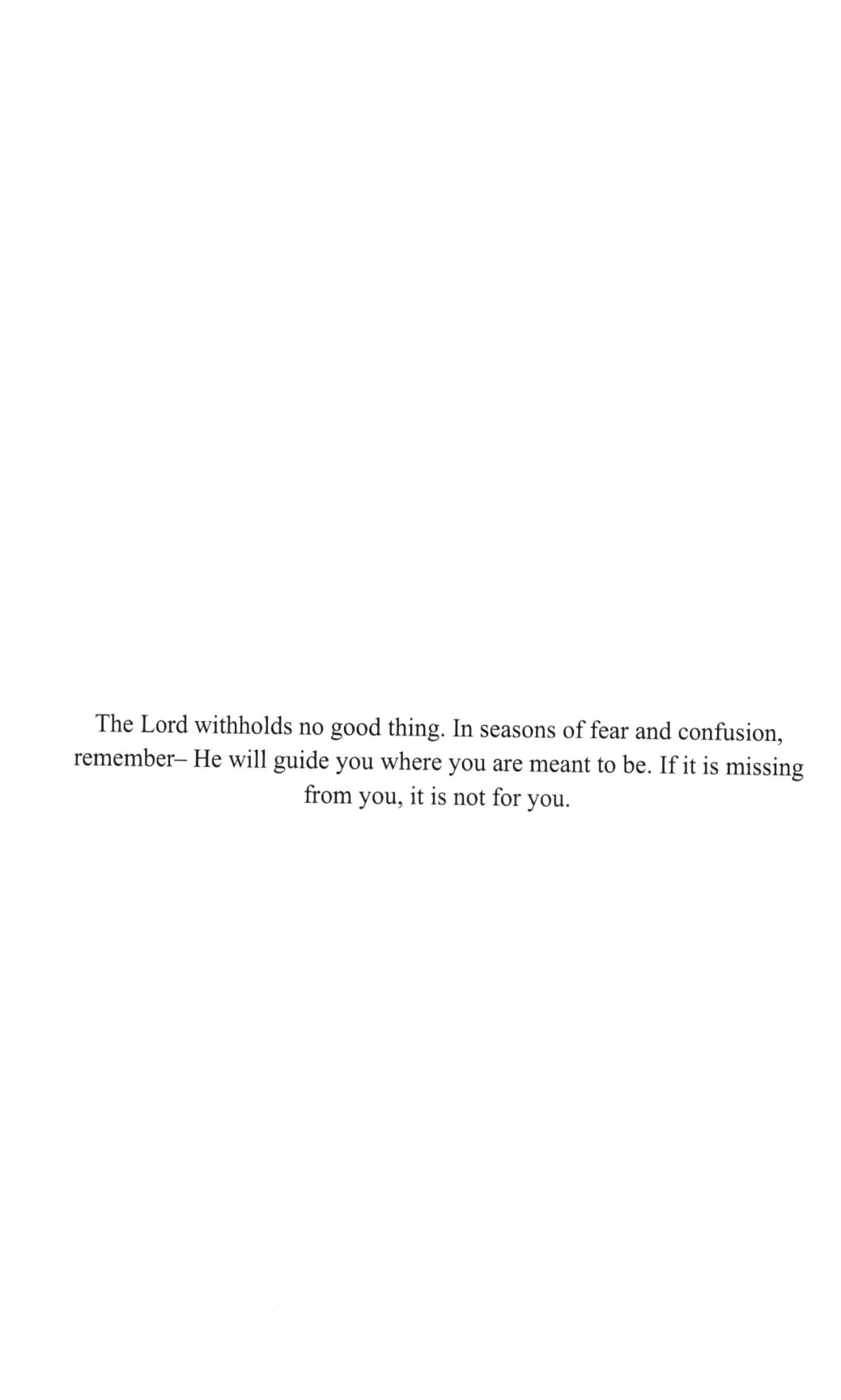

The Lord withholds no good thing. In seasons of fear and confusion, remember– He will guide you where you are meant to be. If it is missing from you, it is not for you.

IF YOU WANT TO LIVE LIFE OUT LOUD – THERE IS NO TIME BUT THE PRESENT! CHASE THE DREAM, THROW THE PARTY, WRITE THE LETTER, CALL THE OLD FLAME. NOTHING IS PROMISED. EVERYTHING IS CHERISHED. WHEN YOU SEEK WISDOM AND HAND OUT GRACE, BEAUTIFUL THINGS WILL COME FROM IT. EAT THE CAKE, DRINK THE WINE, SWIM IN THE OCEAN. YOU DESERVE A LIFE THAT FEELS BEAUTIFUL FROM THE INSIDE OUT.

This is the summer I learned to take care of myself – to bathe myself in kindness and gentleness. I took myself on a long walk on the beach, picking up shells that brought delight to my heart. I devoured book after book on long plane flights and early in the morning at coffee shops. I called my therapist and asked for help. I asked for a hand to stand up. I took myself to church, to time in prayer, to people who loved me. I went to the gym on the days when I wanted to be anywhere else. I journaled when I felt like I had nothing to say but needed to get everything out. It wasn't fun or pretty or play filled but it was worthwhile and holy and honoring.

Dance with me when the moment is right. Or better yet, ask me to dance when the moment couldn't be more wrong. I don't want it when it's convenient only, I want the real stuff, the hard things. I want it all or nothing, baby.

I REMEMBER THE MOMENT I MET YOU AND THOUGHT – THIS PERSON IS GOING TO BE IN MY LIFE FOR ALL OF THE DAYS TO COME. YOUR VERY BEING IS A GIFT TO MY HEART. YOUR WORDS BRING JOY TO MY DAYS. YOUR LAUGH IS MEDICINE. YOUR WAY OF SEEING THE WORLD CHANGED MY LIFE. THANK YOU FOR MAKING ME BETTER WITHOUT EVEN TRYING.

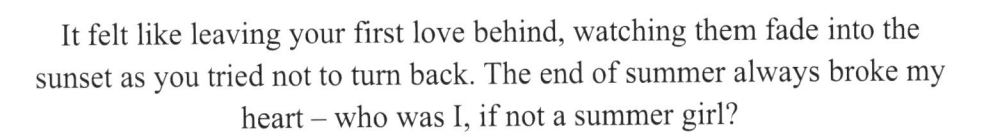

It felt like leaving your first love behind, watching them fade into the sunset as you tried not to turn back. The end of summer always broke my heart – who was I, if not a summer girl?

I parted ways with picnics & tans & swims in the ocean & fresh watermelon & long walks & all the things that pierce my soul with gladness.

I tried earnestly to welcome fall – the cool new friend on the block, waiting around the corner to lure me in. But my heart didn't sing for fall like it did for summer.

I tucked these days away near my heart; I need them when the darkness comes.

Warm yellow hues bathe me in sunlight as I open my eyes. I pull the curtains open a little more, letting the day heal me and take me in. The nights feel lonely and hard and never ending but the mornings are pure bliss. I'm saved by perspective and prayer and journaling and coffee but mostly I'm saved by the quiet moments. There is no other way to start your day than with a glimpse of Heaven above.

August is as bittersweet as losing your first love. It's sharing a sweating bottle of white wine with your crush, passing it back and forth as you watch the sunset. It's the way your legs feel like they are going to give out after a long run in the heat. It's romanticizing your grocery store run and your stop at the post office. It's like giving twenty dollars to the kids on your corner running a lemonade stand. It's the way it feels on Sunday night when you grieve the magical weekend that is slipping behind you. It's the nerves of facing something new, something you dreamed about, and not backing down, even when your hands tremble. It's the smell of the wildflowers in your grandmother's garden and the way it takes you back to your childhood. It's the taste of a popsicle on a Monday night. It's slowing down, letting your time feel as sweet and gentle as honey. It's asking a stranger to sit for a cup of coffee. It's the way it feels to look out the window on a hazy summer night. It's saying goodbye and choking back tears. It's the feeling you get after waking up early and walking to grab coffee and flowers and making it back before anyone else is awake. It's the sound of your body hitting the water after falling off of a surfboard. It's picking up shells on the beach to send in letters to your oldest friends. It's making time for art and love and laughter and play. It's kissing goodbye to another summer, praying it lingers a little longer. August feels like laying on white sheets and taking a long afternoon nap.

Acknowledgements:

Self-published books are no easy thing. It takes a village to do anything, but an even sweeter group to champion you and push you in such an intense creative process.

Thank you to my best friends, near and far, for loving me the way you do. You are the kinds of friends stories are written about. I just love you – Peri, Pornchai, Sam, Darby, Mackenzie, Gigi, Nikki, Bunny, Dea, Eden, Kit, Emily, Jessica, Craig, Sarah, Kaley, Lizzy, Emmie, Mara, Elizabeth, Lauren, Delaney, Madison, Abbey, and so many more. My cup overflows.

I'm indebted forever to my editors– the women who edited this book, loved me and the poems, and who I trust with my writing forever and always. Mom, Audrey, Sarah, Emily, Darby, and Eden – thank you could never mean enough. Thank you to Connor Bowen for my headshot and for being the best photographer I know.

A bouquet of gratitude for Lisa Kleysteuber who kickstarted my art journey when I was a tiny little girl. You are my inspiration for a life well lived.

One big "I love you!" and thank you to all my family on the McCabe and Berry side. You guys are the real deal. I'm so proud to be a part of such big and loving families.

A special note of recognition and honor and absolute adoration to my grandparents – Amma, Ampa, Woo Woo, and CL. You are so much of my heart. You gave me the courage and love to be myself, always. You are my guideposts. We miss you, Amma.

Cj, Audrey, and Aidan– thank God for you three. You are my best friends in this world and nothing makes sense to me unless you are there with me. I could write one million poems about you three and it would barely scratch the surface. I want to be you all when I grow up. Thank you, thank you, I love you.

Mom and Dad – gosh, the English language couldn't have enough words for me to express my gratitude and love for you. You put the word "parent" to shame. You are light to everyone you come across. Your love envelopes me, protects me, and sets me free. I praise God for the gift of being your daughter. Thank you for who you are. I love you, I love you, I love you.